**To you, for planting a seed ...**

By the river was a diligent little piggy named Sanyu, who lived in a stick house with a big banana farm.

E very day, Sanyu tended to the plants: watering, pruning, mulching and fertilizing.

S anyu's pride and passion was to bake the best banana bread around then spread it with tasty homemade banana jam.

Because Sanyu always cooked extra food, there were crates of banana treats secured up in the ceiling.

O n Fridays, Sanyu diligently listed, checked, and organized the food. Each snack had its place.

Whether by inviting friends for a feast or helping others in need, Sanyu loved to share the bounty from those crates. Who would have it any other way?

One day, in the middle of a long drought, Sanyu dedicated all morning to watering the plants. After a while, the ground started forming puddles.

B ut wait, Sanyu didn't pour this much water. The river was overflowing its banks!  Never fear: Sanyu had a plan to deal with floods.

16

Most of the crates were already secured in the ceiling, so Sanyu grabbed some treasured items and climbed to safety.

G radually, the waters drained. Sanyu would need to buy more supplies and build new walls, but thankfully there was plenty of food safely in storage.

Hold on, it looked like people were coming down the road... Sanyu's friends were here to help!

With so many hard-working hands,
Sanyu's team repaired every twig
of the house in no time.

The very next night, Sanyu hosted a feast to celebrate safety, friendship, food, and good health for all.

This is where years of hard work
and preparation truly paid off.  It was
like Mama Piggy's wise old saying...

"Even though the future is uncertain, you can always prepare for a brighter tomorrow. What you save is what you earn, and those who give will also receive."

Hello from Eli! You know that warm, fuzzy feeling when somebody is nice to you? If we save what we can and then give it to those in need, we get to help others have that special feeling in a big way-  just like when Sanyu had enough to share!  It is always important to build strong foundations like savings, food supplies, and community support... these can help you rebuild after a disaster.